Aging
American Style

by

Lynn Zacny Busby

Cover Art
Old-goat Image by Clker-Free-Vector-Images from Pixabay. Pixabay License is free for commercial use; no attribution required.

Notice:
Any products or company names used throughout this book have not been solicited. The author has not received any compensation for their use.

Intro and credits

I married my husband, Bob Busby, because he made me laugh. We are now going on 40 years and he's still at it.

This book was made possible by gleaning many of his observations on life.

In addition to my husband, I wish to thank Jana Dube Hletko and Ellen Zacny for editing.

The art/photo contributors of Pixabay. Pixabay.com is a collection of wonderful artwork and photos contributed by professionals and pre-approved to be used commercially. Each graphic is numbered and the artist is identified in the Endnotes.

Favorite quotes

There is a thin line that separates laughter and pain, comedy and tragedy, humor and hurt.
Erma Bombeck

Sometimes you gotta laugh to keep from cryin'.
Vinis Zacny

Inside every cynical person there's a disappointed idealist.
George Carlin

Don't let old age get you down; it's too hard to get back up.
John Wagner

It's always somethin'.
Gilda Radner

Table of contents

Becoming old has its advantages

*1

No more Mondays

*2

I find retirement is like my teen years only better because I own a car and have a steady boyfriend. I have plenty of free time, and I'm not required to show up anywhere in the morning. I can join a group of friends to go out socially with no curfew.

Retirement is good.

Grandparenting really is grand

One of the best parts of aging is becoming a grandparent! As a grandparent, I delight in having the time to watch little ones play and learn.
And when it's time for **my** nap, I can just send them home.

*3

Incontinence and edema

*4

As I get older, my insides have started to loosen up. With less bladder control comes incontinence, but with my weakened heart comes fluid retention.

Problem solved.

You can't lose with comfy shoes

*5

Long ago I traded my color coordinated stilettos for comfy shoes though now my color choices are limited (dirty white or newly purchased white.)

Who moved my keys?

Every time I can't find something, I'm sure someone moved it. If you're empty nested, the suspect list is pretty narrow.

It's different when I can't remember why I went into a room or what I'm looking for, but I have a fix:

I just go into a room, pull up a chair, and wait until I need something.

*6

Cereal

*7

I never did like cooking – the time required preparing didn't seem like a good investment in my future.

Thankfully, I have discovered that cereal alone works just fine to keep one alive.

Readers jeepers

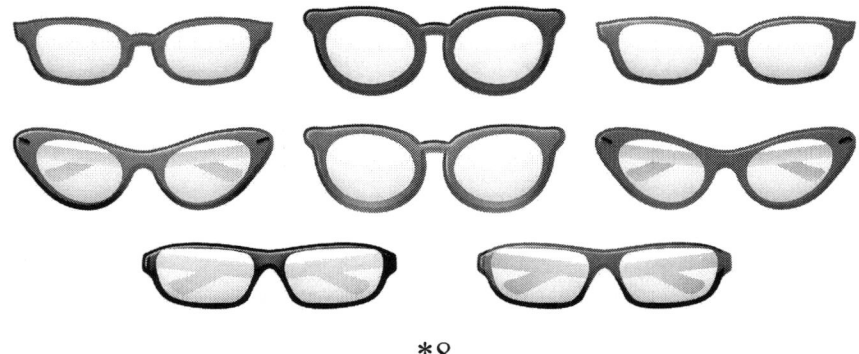

*8

I find that having a pair of magnifying readers on every flat surface in the house is a real time saver.

Since I don't need to go from room to room searching for my glasses anymore, this allows me the freedom to go *au naturel* between readings.

The olden daze

*9

I don't think dementia is at all as bad as it sounds - it can even be fun and frugal.

For example, I haven't bought a new book or movie in years.

Staying positive

I try hard to be an optimist. For example the other day I fell down the stairs and instead of getting upset I thought, "Wow, that's the fastest I've moved in years."

*10

Aging has a few downsides

*11

Creepy, crappy, crepey skin

I first noticed this phenomenon when reaching up to turn off the bed light and allowing my eyes to focus on my forearm. Suddenly I had alligator skin. Does anyone think an alligator is attractive? Other alligators? ...Maybe?

*12

Wrinkles are the life lines of the face

*13

Wrinkles on men say wisdom,

Wrinkles on men say sage,

Wrinkles on women say,
"What's it to ya?"

Thin hair? Where?

*14

I first noticed my thinning hair while driving my car in the daytime. I looked in the rear view mirror and could see daylight through the top of my head hair.

Was it a thyroid problem? A hormone problem? A worry problem? A stress problem?

No, just a problem of still caring what my hair looked like.

Sensory deception

One minute I'm young and fun and the next, I'm turning down the stereo in my car to see better.

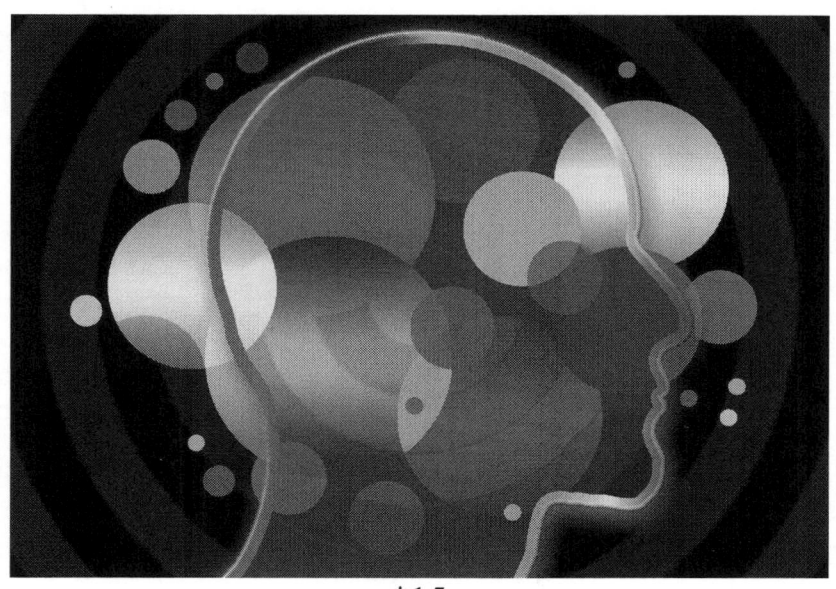
*15

Driving diva

*16

I don't always go the extra mile, but when I do it's because I missed my exit.[a]

When to stop driving?

*17

Not only did I notice more scratches on the car, but I started running my walker into furniture in the house.

That's when I knew it was time to stop driving and ride shotgun.

Memory issue

I thought wisdom was supposed to offset the physical drawbacks of aging, but it seems I was wrong again.

I should have a lot of knowledge from years of education and experience, but it seems my indexer is missing some pieces.

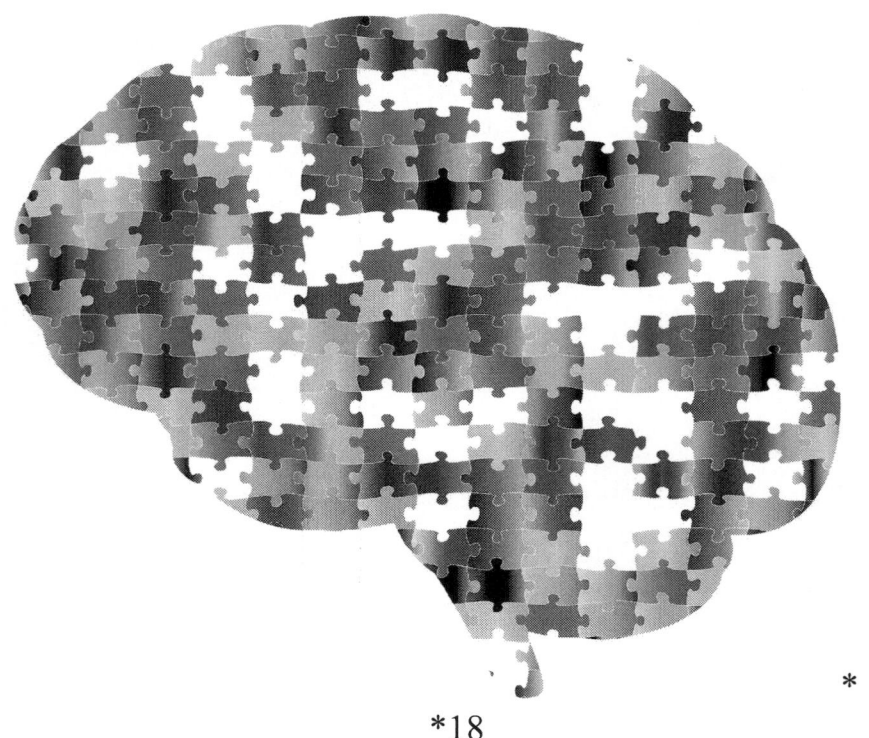

*18

*

26

Short term memory

*19

A friend recently asked if I could keep a secret.

I said, "Sure, no problem.
…What did you say?"

These wheels are made for walkin'

*20

When natural ambulation starts to fail, a walker is the answer - six legs are always better than two.

But even with a walker, I must still provide direction and forward motion. Someone needs to put a seat and a motor ...oh, ... wait... never mind.

Money matters

I think I have saved enough money to live in the style to which I have become accustomed.

If not, I plan to perk up my Purina with a little parsley.

*21

Jack Sprat

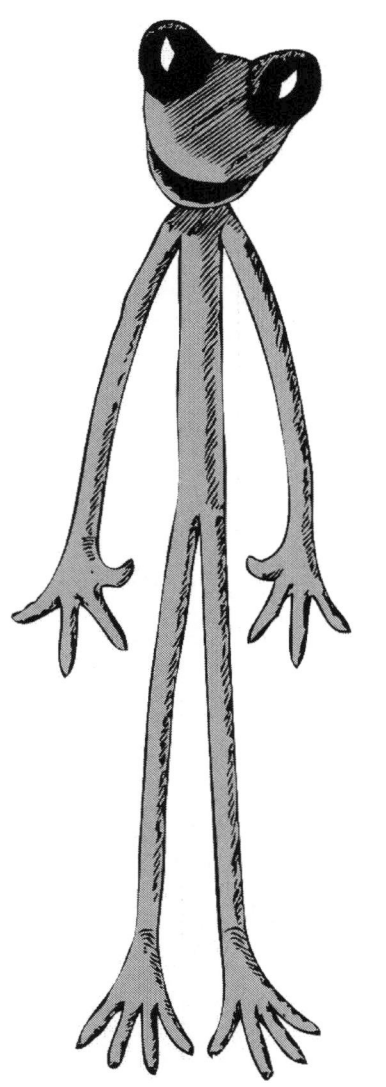

Jack Sprat was clearly a fairy tale.

There are no skinny **old** people!

I'm just going to write off my obesity to genetics and go have ice cream.

*22

So long

*23

A friend told me a by-product of significant weight gain is that the penis tends to recede into a fat roll and is no longer visible from the owner's point of view.

Bye, bye little feller.

Stair care

According to the NCIH, approximately one-third of community-dwelling, healthy adults aged 65 years and over fall at least once per year.[b]

It is rumored that in his later years, even though it cramped his dancing style, Fred Astaire used the handrail.

*24

Fear of falling

*25

As mentioned, falling is a big concern for the elderly.

A friend shared with me that there comes a time when a man starts to fear tripping over his own balls.

Elderly nakedness

*26

When elderly, naked is that time between robe to shower to towel and should be as short as possible.

Arthur Ritis takes up residence

*27

My mother-in-law suffered from arthritis but called it Arthur Ritis. She said "The bastard comes and goes as he pleases and is a lousy guest."

Even with her buckled knuckles, she managed a round of Tylenol with a rum chaser.

Dem bones, dem bones, dem damn bones

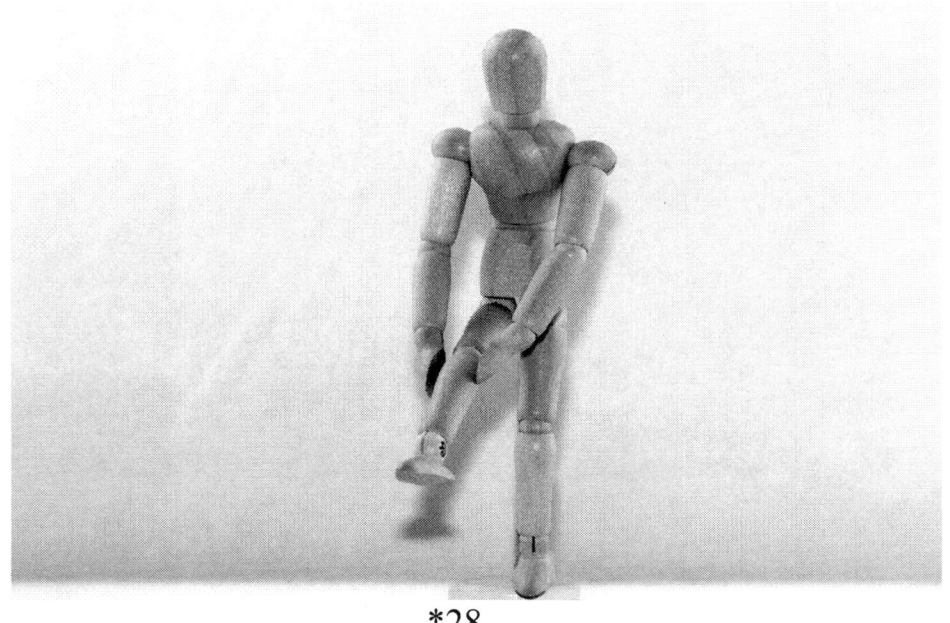
*28

For a car, if only the brake shoes are bad, why replace the whole brake?   Why do surgeons want to replace the whole joint when only the padding is worn?

For me, the bright side of the COVID-19 period is that self-quarantine requires dramatically less need to walk anywhere and thus I cancelled my knee surgery.

Waddling

*29

Waddle is an ugly word for people whether referring to walk style or neck pile.

Plantar fasciitis is not in the solar system

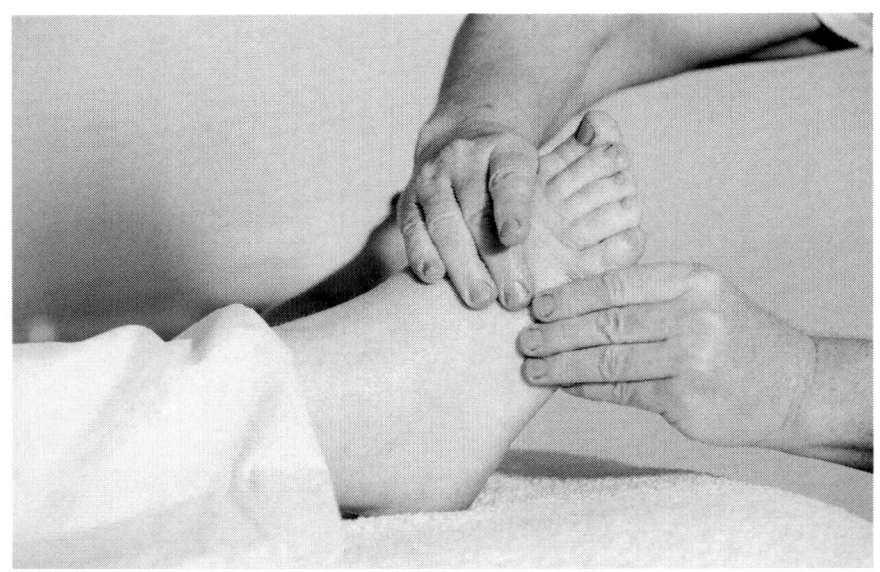

*30

Plantar means bottom of the foot.

Fasciitis means painful as hell.

Addressing pain

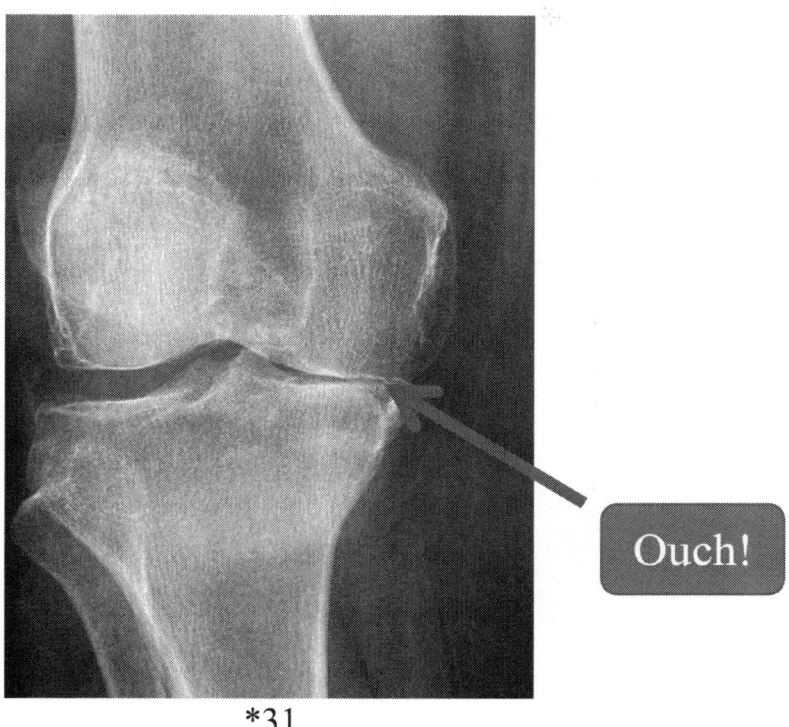

*31

I find that plenty of aspirin is a fix for headache, backpain, knee pain and all of it because it leaves me with a hole in my stomach which detracts from the other issues.

Nailed it

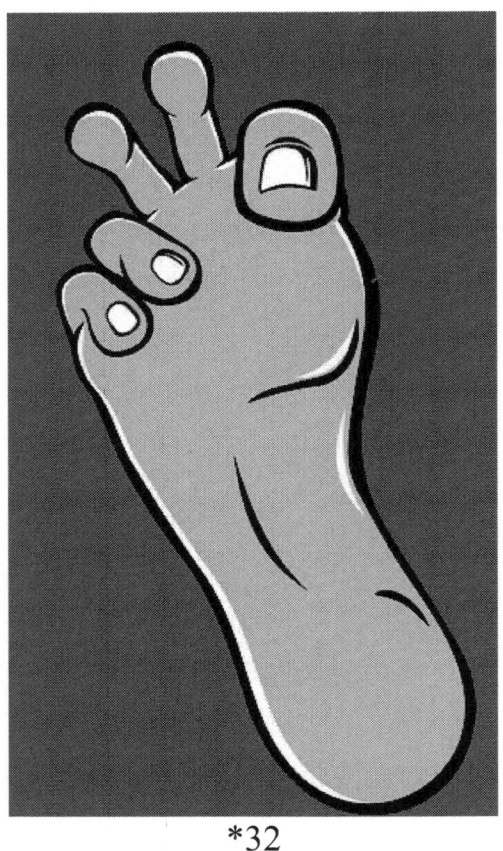

*32

We signed a prenuptial agreement
which contains a paragraph that specifies that
we stay together in sickness and in health so
long as that did not include trimming the
other's toenails.

Hang on boobie, boobie hang on

*33

So what if my boobs have decided to droop
With no possibility to ever recoup
Let 'em swing
Let 'em sway
I'm going braless as of today

Easy bruising

Because his skin has thinned so much my husband now gets red/purple patches on his arms so easily that I'm afraid to let him out in a rain storm.

*34

Out, out damned spot

*35

According to the New York Post, women in the USA spend around $3,000 on cosmetics annually. This translates to around $225,360 throughout their entire lifetime.

Ironically, most of that money is spent in vain.

Hot tip for back pain

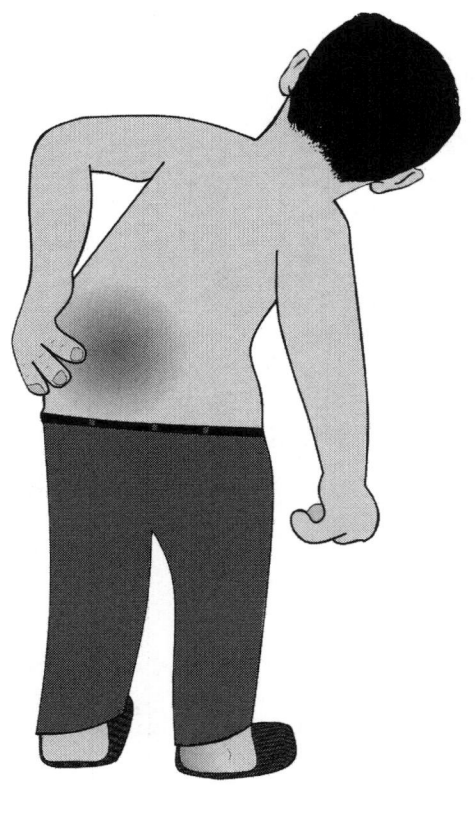

*36

A heating pad may help an aching back; however, be advised that my husband says it works best if turned on.

Medical staff

*37

I look forward to doctor visits now.
I'm desperate for social contact.

How did that happen?

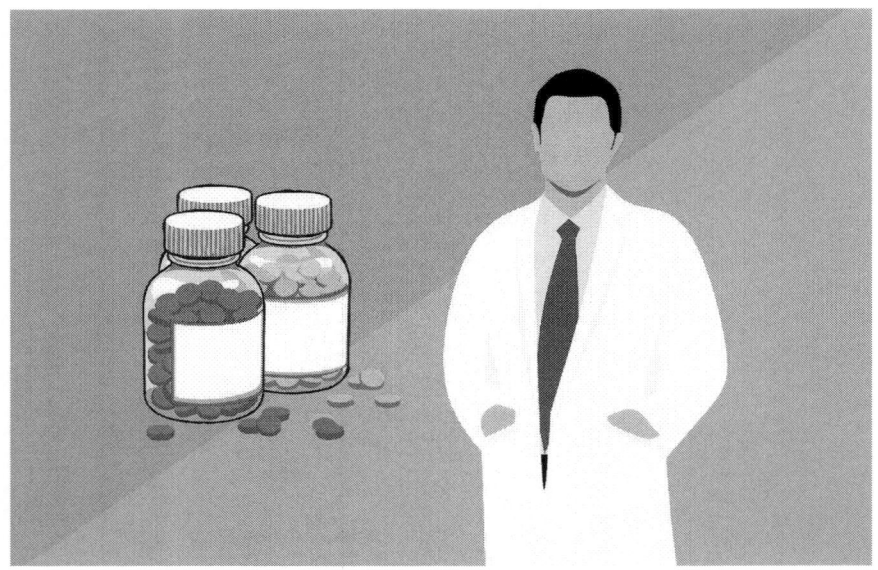

*38

How is it that one day you are young, even athletic, and then suddenly you have a favorite pharmacy?

Pricey tags

Skin tags are painless but ugly. You can have them taken off individually, but that can get pricey.

It makes more sense, as Billy Crystal suggested, that after the age of 50, the body needs to be regularly sand blasted.

*39

Coffee is vital for survival

*40

Dinosaurs didn't have coffee,
and look how that turned out.。

Universal observations

*41

The curse of clumsiness

*42

I find that yelling and cussing is markedly increased in my house during our senior years.

Quantity is in direct proportion to the number of things that don't work as they should, the number of spills, and the number of contacts with walls, doors, and cabinets.

Don't lose controls

*43

Lost remote,
wrong remote,
and "dysfunctional" remote
are root causes of elderly profanity.

Mirror, mirror

*44

Too often I get up in the morning, look at myself in the mirror and think…

"No, that can't be right."

Thinning eyebrows

*45

The nice thing about disappearing eyebrows is that with a clean slate, it's easier to draw them on anyway you like.

Outgrown hair

I have recently noticed new hairs growing from my chin which I call wandering eyebrows.

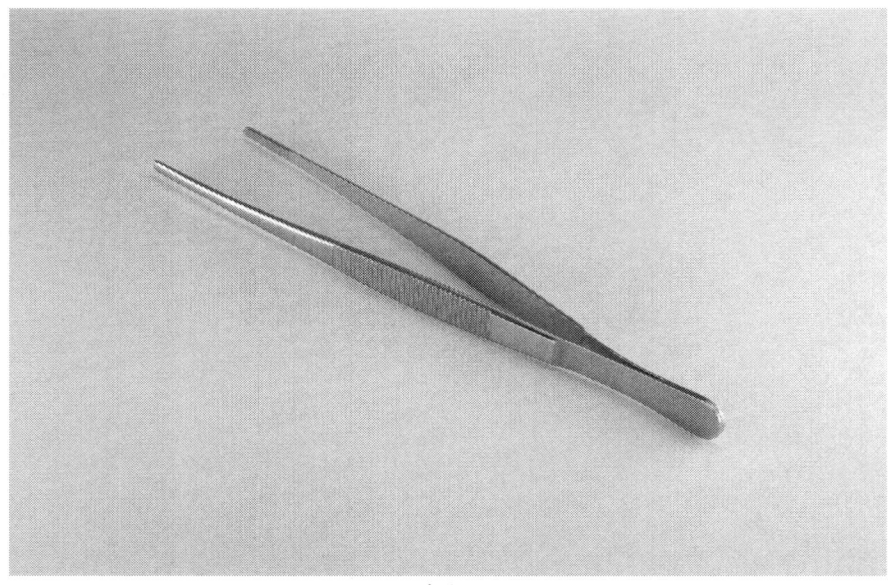

*46

Wild hair

When a guy starts running into things on a regular basis, it's time to consider trimming the eyebrows.

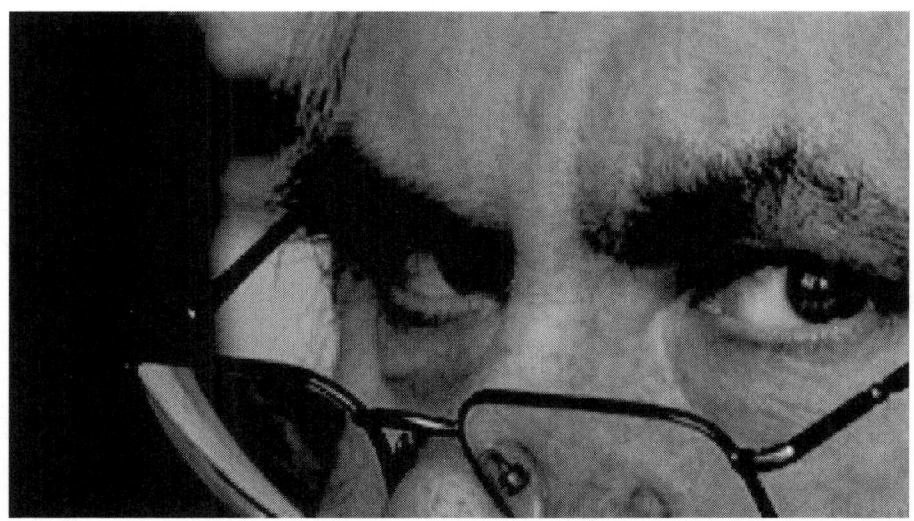

Surprise sphincter shutdown

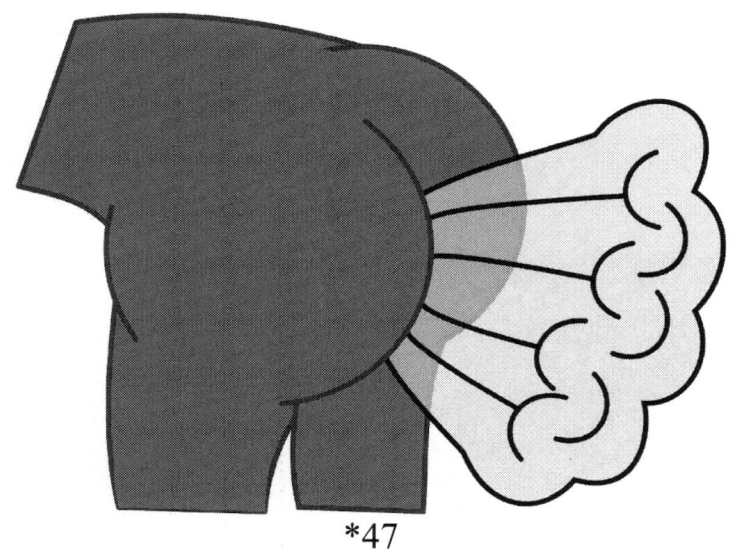

*47

My sphincter is no longer reliable and cannot be trusted. I must decide whether to apologize and draw attention to the mishap or just shame the dog?

Note: it is presumed that all seniors have a dog for this purpose.

(See: Senior Rescue)

Senior rescue

*48

Pets are good for companions during our later years.

If you don't already have a dog, you will need one. An older rescue dog is preferred as s/he will likely offer more camouflaging smells.

(See: Surprise sphincter shutdown)

Traveling pains

Every morning requires an inventory of what parts are and are not working for that day.

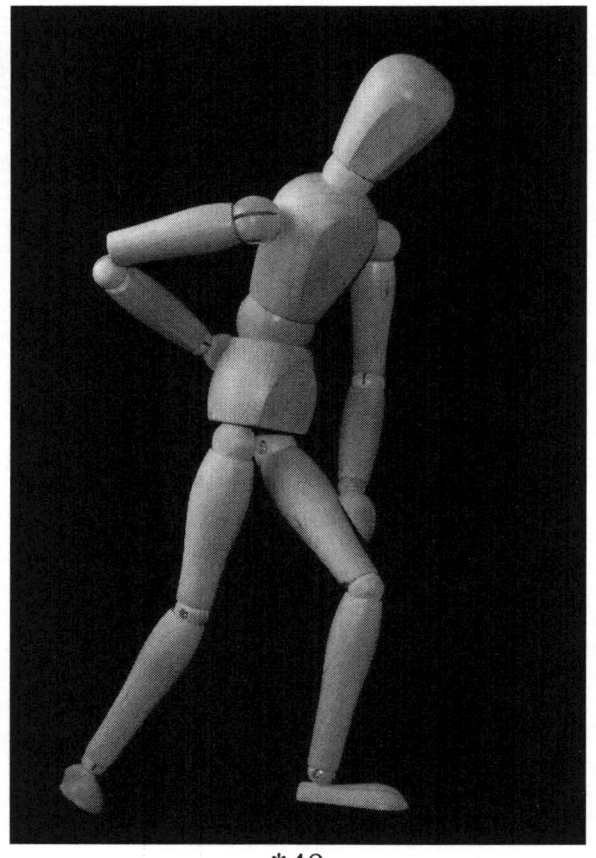

*49

Note: traveling pains often run concurrent with Grumpy Gramps.

Back up

Who knew there would come a time when you'd rather have a good bowel movement than good sex?

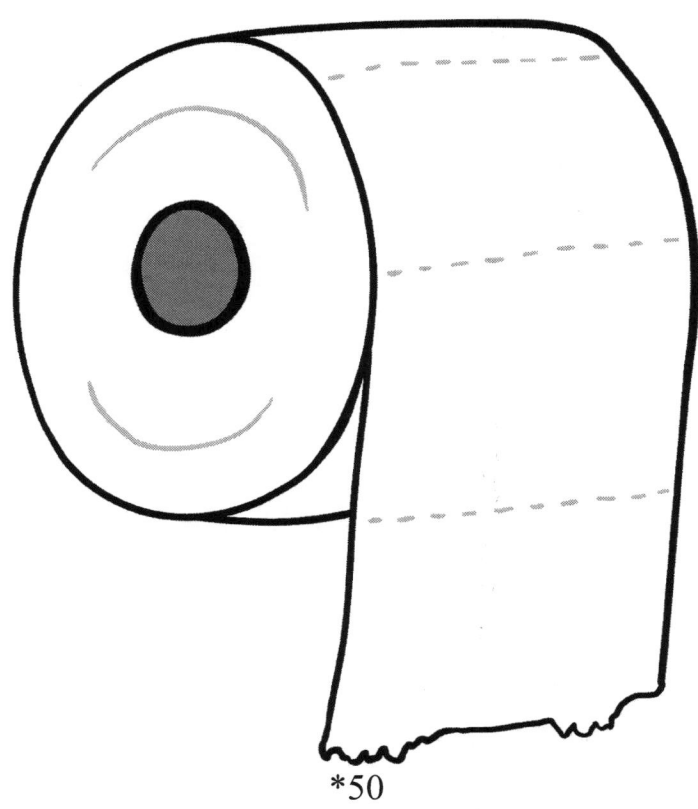

*50

Censure dentures

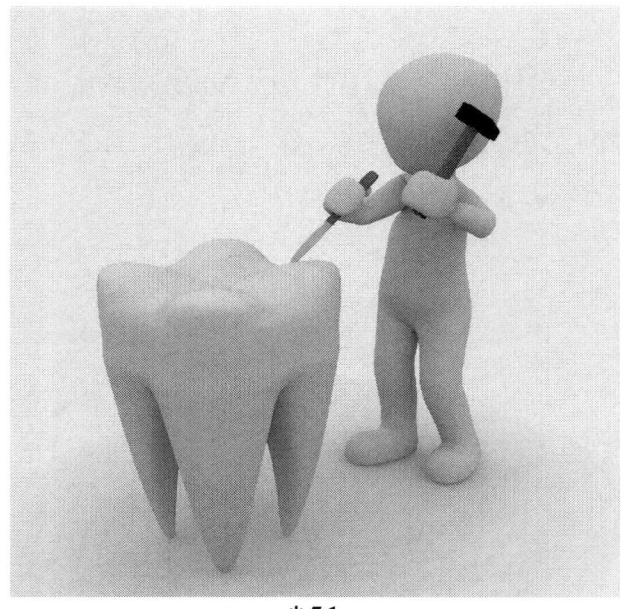

*51

I have had several root canals and capped teeth, so I assumed there is nothing left to decay and thus dental bills would be over.

Ney, ney. I got decay inside a capped root canal which was treated by doing another root canal <u>through</u> a cap --- all for the price of a good set of dentures.

DadGUM it!

*52

Even with no cavity in years, I am now subject to receding gums which can expose the root of the tooth and cause severe pain.

Isn't that a bite!

Errant hair

My husband experiences errant hair growth in his ears.

Thankfully, his ears are growing larger to allow for the new growth.

*53

Patience

*54

As I get older, I don't have the patience I used to.
It seems I just don't have time for it.

Insomnia

My husband doesn't get to sleep until after 3:00 AM, and gets up late; I go to bed earlier and wake up earlier.

Having our own quiet time I believe to be the reason we have had a long and joyful marriage.

That, and he cooks.

*55

Lennon lapse

*56

My husband and I recently watched the movie *Rocketman* and there is a scene where Elton chooses his stage surname.

When asked, he looked at a picture of the Beatles on the wall and responded: John.

Paul McCartney, Ringo Starr, George Harrison,
and John… John…John… John
… 2 syllables…
Ah crap!

Just a matter of time

*57

Whether it is a missing word, forgetting a skill, or doing a Google search, it seems to take me longer to do everything and I'm not even sure if I got it right any way.

I have found one of the hardest things to adjust to as I age is getting used to incompetence.

Health tips

*58

The answer to a long life

*59

George Burns, the comedian who lived to be 100, was once asked:

"What is the secret to old age?"

His reply: "Stay warm."

Leverage your position

When I fall and hit the floor, I take advantage of the situation and look around – I recently found two nickels and some leftover Halloween candy.

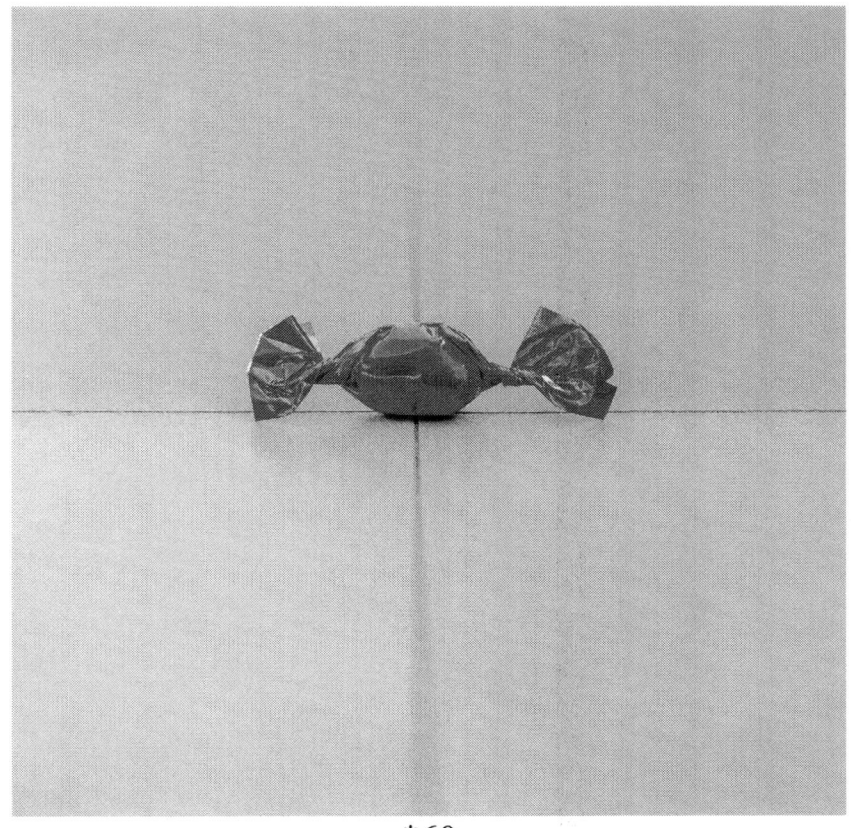

*60

Be grateful

The best advice from my mother to find happiness was simply "Be grateful."

It is not a cure for unhappiness but allows time for reflection.

(See: It could always be worse)

*61

It could always be worse

*d

I feel sorry for baboons but they lessen my concern about hemorrhoids.

Make new friends

*62

As we grow older our inventory of friends naturally grows smaller.

With this in mind, I'm always on the lookout for interesting acquaintances.

Take naps

*63

I am finding more need to rest between vigorous activities like loading the dishwasher or unloading the dryer.

Warm up

Exercise for my husband is not an option. He has to sit on the edge of the bed and warm up like an old Buick before he can get up.

Caretaker or care taker

*64

Does it mean that…

As we age, we need more care?

or

As we age, some of us still care?

I dunno, …but take care now.

Time saver

The deluxe double decker pill holder allows me to avoid wasting time opening my multiple medicine bottles on a daily basis.

I feel it is important to steal time wherever I can.

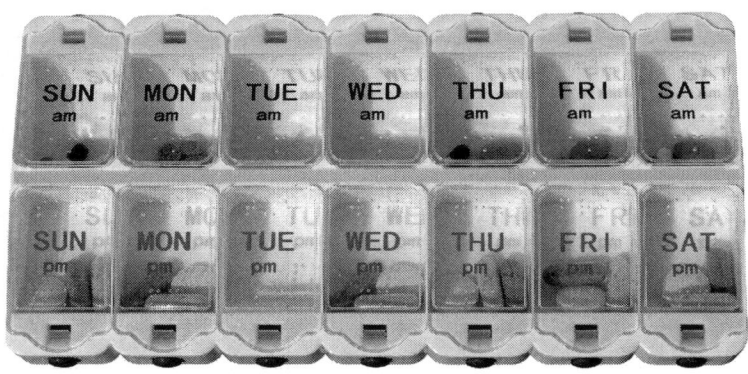

*65

Contusion or confusion

*66

Anyone with a past head injury will want to document it for future excuse making when you put the cereal box in the refrigerator.

Surgery perjury

Get a group of old people together and there will be talk of ailments and surgery. Who had the longest surgery, who had the best surgeon, etc.

*67

Who knew we would be talking about old scar stories?

And vertigo for all

It is not uncommon for me to experience a feeling that the room is spinning.

I've learned to just relax and enjoy the ride.

*68

Stretching Exercise

*69

I walk 5 miles a day.

Actually, that's quite a stretch.

Hit the deck

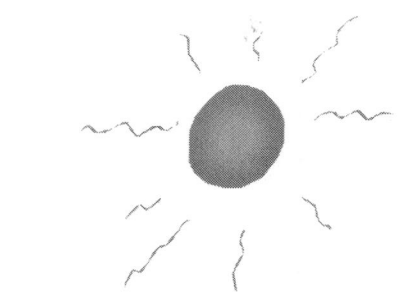

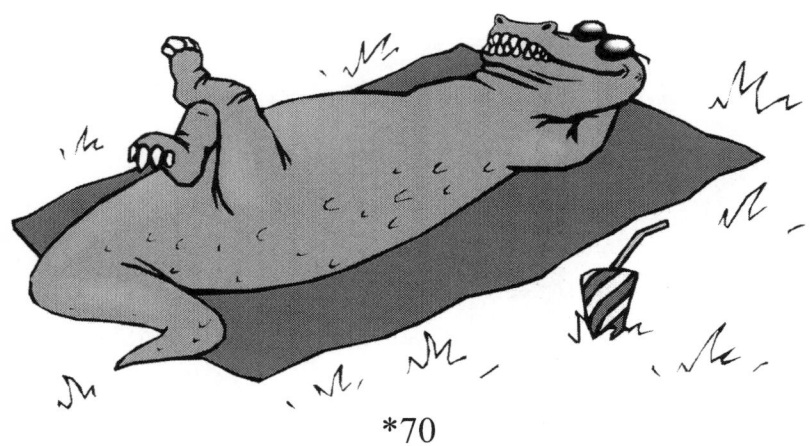

*70

My doctor prescribed Vitamin D.

I call it my afternoon delight.

Help - I've shrunk...

Osteoporosis affects both sexes. It can cause you to shrink up to two inches.

Men tend to be annoyed by it, but it's great for women who always wanted to be on the top of a cheerleading pyramid.

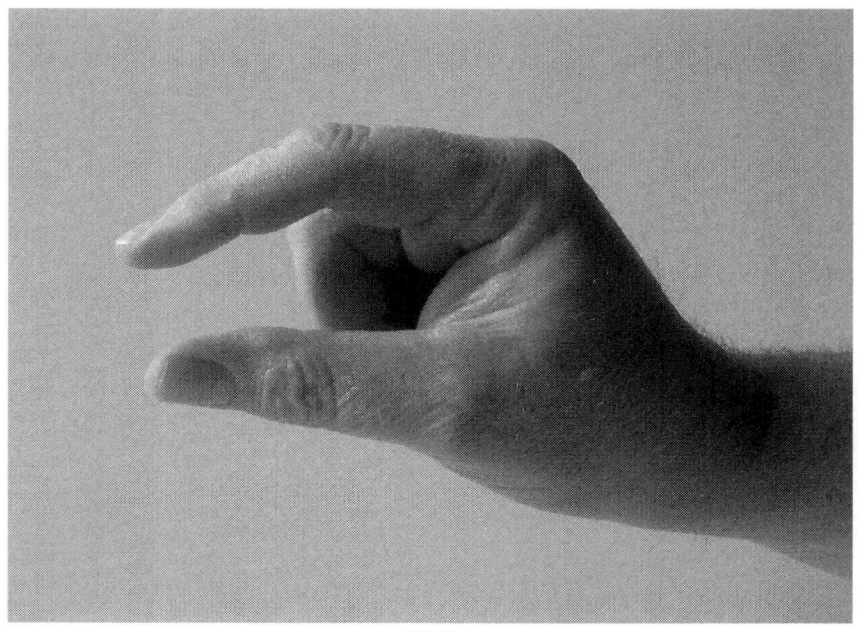
*71

Cortizone

*72

I've had the shot, but frankly,
my daily double neat does a better jo
to put me in the zone.

Dr. Google

*73

With every new symptom, I get on my computer and do a Google search to self-diagnose my ailment.

I'm always sure to tell my GP about my findings...doctors love that.

Hobbies and pastimes

*74

Boozin' and loosin'

I stay away from using alcohol to pass the time or cure the blues. I worry I might start whining:

"Poor me, poor me, pour me another drink."

*75

Technology time

*76

After 40 years each in the computer industry, my husband and I have lost many of our technical skills.

He can still program the remote, but if he dies before me, I will have to leave the TV on whatever channel was playing at the time.

Netflix and kill

I watch mysteries to try to keep my mind sharp.

I also use them as research should I ever feel the need to eliminate my full time roommate.

*77

Try something new

*78

George H.W. Bush celebrated his 90th birthday by skydiving.

Though to be fair, it wasn't his first time.

Mountaineering

Some activities may be out of bounds for me.

I see people around my age mountain climbing. I feel good getting my leg through my underwear without losing my balance.

*79

Pastime - gardening

*80

Gardening is different than most hobbies in that something useful can come from it.

Pastime - music

Music soothes the savage beast,
or
makes you forget about it at least.

*81

Pastime - sewing

*82

An old sewing machine is a nice thing to have around as a reminder that some really old things can still function.

Pastime - cooking

Retirement is a great time to learn to cook. However, I have found that when I add wine directly to the chef, I end up feeling _sous_ lousy the next day.

*83

Pastime - fishing

*84

I like to work smart. I feel I increase my chance of success by limiting the fish to a relatively small space.

Pastime - gaming

I recommend games that offer a mental challenge.

*85

Pastime - reading

Some people read for pleasure.

I read as a sleep aid, but that does seem to reduce my retention.

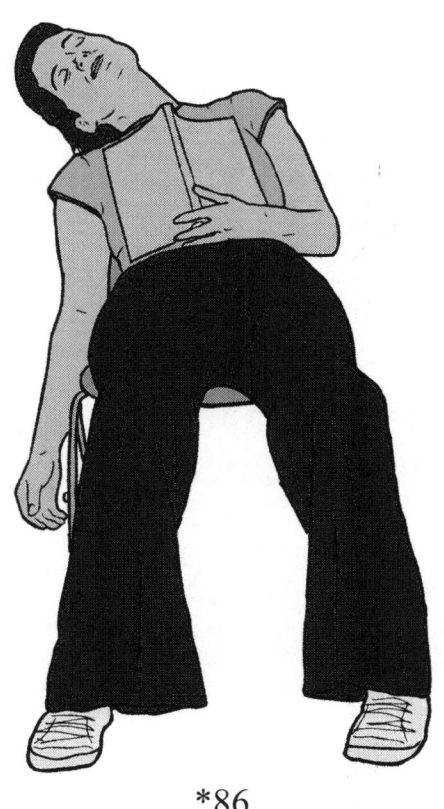

*86

Pastime - collecting

*87

I have several collections so as to fill the house with worthless treasures for my children to dispose of.

(See Estate planning)

Pastime - cake decorating

I got into cake decorating a couple of years ago and, as with all good hobbies, it held my interest until I had purchased every possible item in support of it.

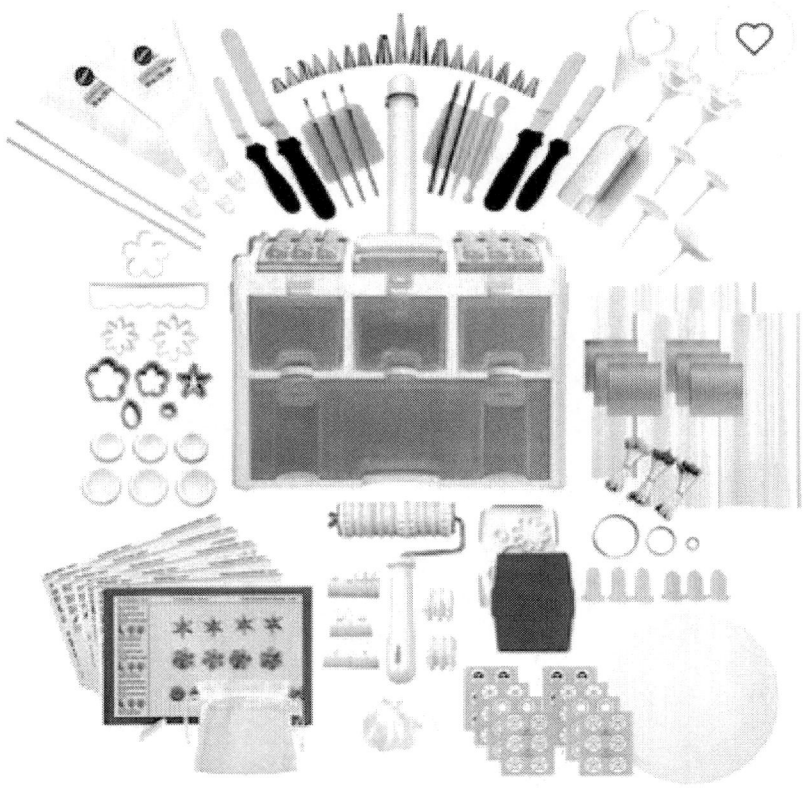

(See: Estate planning)

Estate planning

*88

I'm sure my children dread my death. It means they will have the headache of getting rid of all my stuff.

Bob refers to our basement as "Lynn's indoor landfill."

Spend like there's no tomorrow

*89

Beat heirs to the punch - go ahead and buy that vacation you always wanted.

Can't travel? NP. Go on the internet and buy trinkets from all the places you can't go.

(See: Estate Planning)

If I had a hammer
I'd give it to Jimmy Carter

*g

It was because of Jimmy Carter that I realized I have no skill to offer for the good of humanity so I decided to write this book instead.

Graphics reference legend

Below please find references for the numbers used to identify the graphics contained in this book from https://pixabay.com

Stunning free images & royalty free stock
Over 1.8 million+ high quality stock images and videos shared by our talented community.

Notice:

Any products or company names used throughout this book have not been solicited. The author has not received any compensation for their use.

¹ Image by Clker-Free-Vector-Images from Pixabay
² Image by Gerd Altmann from Pixabay
³ Image by KERBSTONE from Pixabay
⁴ Image by Juanita Mulder from Pixabay
⁵ Image by Clker-Free-Vector-Images from Pixabay
⁶ Image by kalhh from Pixabay
⁷ Image by kannojiashreyak from Pixabay
⁸ Image by Annalise Batista from Pixabay
⁹ Image by Prawny from Pixabay
¹⁰ Image by Gerd Altmann from Pixabay
¹¹ Image by Gerd Altmann from Pixabay
¹² Image by Susanne Jutzeler, suju-foto from Pixabay
¹³ Image by OpenClipart-Vectors from Pixabay
¹⁴ Image by Efes Kitap from Pixabay
¹⁵ Image by Gerd Altmann from Pixabay
¹⁶ Image by Clker-Free-Vector-Images from Pixabay
¹⁷ Image by Jan Helebrant from Pixabay
¹⁸ Image by Gordon Johnson from Pixabay
¹⁹ Image by Gerd Altmann from Pixabay
²⁰ Image by Ladislava Vantuchová from Pixabay
²¹ Image by Gerd Altmann from Pixabay
²² Image by Clker-Free-Vector-Images from Pixabay
²³ Image by Clker-Free-Vector-Images from Pixabay
²⁴ Image by mohamed Hassan from Pixabay
²⁵ Image by OpenIcons from Pixabay
²⁶ Image by Peggy und Marco Lachmann-Anke from Pixabay
²⁷ Image by Alexas_Fotos from Pixabay
²⁸ Image by Wolfgang Claussen from Pixabay
²⁹ Image by Clker-Free-Vector-Images from Pixabay
³⁰ Image by andreas160578 from Pixabay
³¹ mage by Dr. Manuel González Reyes from Pixabay
³² Image by Alexander Lesnitsky from Pixabay
³³ Image by SilviaP_Design from Pixabay
³⁴ Image by OpenClipart-Vectors from Pixabay
³⁵ Image by Dmitry Abramov from Pixabay
³⁶ Image by Christian Dorn from Pixabay

[37] *Image by Niran Kasri from Pixabay*

[38] *Image by mohamed Hassan from Pixabay*

[39] *Image by Miguel Á. Padriñán from Pixabay*

[40] *Image by Vinson Tan (楊祖武) from Pixabay*

[41] *Image by Luc Mahler from Pixabay*

[42] *Image by Steve Buissinne from Pixabay*

[43] *Image by tookapic from Pixabay*

[44] *Image by Andre Mouton from Pixabay*

[45] *Image by Chrystal Elizabeth from Pixabay*

[46] *Image by HeungSoon from Pixabay*

[47] *Image by OpenClipart-Vectors from Pixabay*

[48] *Image by labsafeharbor from Pixabay*

[49] *Image by Wolfgang Claussen from Pixabay*

[50] *Image by b0red from Pixabay*

[51] *Image by Peggy und Marco Lachmann-Anke from Pixabay*

[52] *Image by OpenClipart-Vectors from Pixabay*

[53] *Image by David Mark from Pixabay*

[54] *Image by OpenClipart-Vectors from Pixabay*

[55] *Image by Irina Savchishina from Pixabay*

[56] *Image by pauldaley1977 from Pixabay*

[57] *Image by chenspec from Pixabay*

[58] *Image by Gordon Johnson from Pixabay*

[59] *Image by Free-Photos from Pixabay*

[60] *Image by Franck Barske from Pixabay*

[61] *Image by Clker-Free-Vector-Images from Pixabay*

[62] *Image by Claudia Peters from Pixabay*

[63] *Image by Ralf Designs from Pixabay*

[64] *Image by Santa3 from Pixabay*

[65] *Image by Kevin Phillips from Pixabay*

[66] *Image by Sarah Peets from Pixabay*

[67] *Image by OpenClipart-Vectors from Pixabay*

[68] *Image by Manfred Antranias Zimmer from Pixabay*

[69] *Image by Alexas_Fotos from Pixabay*

[70] *Image by Clker-Free-Vector-Images from Pixabay*

[71] *Image by Gerd Altmann from Pixabay*

[72] *Image by Clker-Free-Vector-Images from Pixabay*

[73] *Image by Abhilash Jacob from Pixabay*

[74] *Image by Wolfgang Eckert from Pixabay .jpg*
[75] *Image by OpenClipart-Vectors from Pixabay*
[76] *Image by Ron Porter from Pixabay*
[77] *Image by OpenClipart-Vectors from Pixabay*
[78] *Image by Clker-Free-Vector-Images from Pixabay*
[79] *Image by Alemko Coksa from Pixabay*
[80] *Image by Clker-Free-Vector-Images from Pixabay*
[81] *Image by Luc Mahler from Pixabay*
[82] *Image by Pexels from Pixabay*
[83] *Image by Alexas_Fotos from Pixabay*
[84] *Image by OpenClipart-Vectors from Pixabay*
[85] *Image by Reinhold Silbermann from Pixabay*
[86] *Image by Clker-Free-Vector-Images from Pixabay*
[87] *Image by Mahua Sarkar from Pixabay*
[88] *Image by Mediamodifier from Pixabay*
[89] *Image by Olya Adamovich from Pixabay*

Other source references

[a] Page 22 Oldtimers Facebook page as of 9/5/2020
https://www.facebook.com/OldtimersPage/photos/a.159447634399831/1344249102586339/

[b] Page 31 Study source as of 9/5/2020
https://www.ncbi.nlm.nih.gov/books/NBK305246/

[c] Page 47 Oldtimers Facebook page as of 9/5/2020
https://www.facebook.com/OldtimersPage/posts/1347001345644448

[d] Page 71 Photo source as of 9/5/2020
http://fun2shhworld.blogspot.com/2011/05/latest-baboon-animal-wallpapers.html

[e] Page 74 Oldtimers Facebook as of 9/5/2020
https://www.facebook.com/OldtimersPage/photos/a.159447634399831/1347014025643180/

[f] Page 89 Old timers Facebook page as of 9/5/2020
https://www.facebook.com/OldtimersPage/posts/1102945436716708

[g] Page 101 Carter Photo Source as of 9/5/2020
https://www.ajc.com/news/jimmy-carter-picking-hammer-once-again-build-habitat-homes/gXp4onjTB48toZWjCb6b7J/